MW01247075

THE GIFT

of Thanks

THE GIFT of Thanks

BRIEF REFLECTIONS ON GRATITUDE

MARGARET BERNARD

DREAM
RELEASER
PUBLISHING

Acknowledgments

I thank God for the Holy Spirit who inspired and empowered me to write this book. I thank Mr. John Schondelmayer and his team for giving me the tools to bring this book to fruition.

I dedicate this book to my family. To the Matriarch of our family—my mother, Diana Crichlow—who is a pillar of strength in the family. She instilled in me a spiritual foundation that taught me how to trust God.

To my sister, Cherrol-Crichlow Bernard, who has always supported me.

To my adult sons, Mark Bernard and Marlon Bernard, who are the loves of my life.

To my husband Victor E. Bernard, my brother, Lionel Crichlow, and my dad, Denis Crichlow, the men who love me dearly.

January 1st

Today is a new day, and I just want to say thank you, God, for gracing me with life to see it. You are so kind and loving to me, and I thank you for this new year where I get to begin again on a new page!

January 2nd

Lord, thank you for waking me up
this morning. I have the use of my
five senses, and I'm in my right mind.
Thank you for your grace, mercy, and
loving-kindness towards me. Thank
you for salvation, and the freedom to
worship you freely. I'm so grateful.

January 3rd

Lord, thank you for making my workload easy. I thought that I would've been overwhelmed with so many things, but your grace was sufficient. Thank you, Lord, for your grace.

January 4th

What a joy it is to be thankful, Lord!
Each day I find joy in thanking you
for the little things like bending
my elbow and knee and blinking
my eye. There is a tendency to
take these things for granted,
and I just want to say thank you,
Lord, for the ability to use them.

January 5th

Lord, thank you for this day. Use me today to bless someone, to speak a word of encouragement, and to bring your name glory by putting a smile on their face.

January 6th

It's a privilege to be alive! Thank you, God, for your faithfulness every waking moment. Some are in their graves today, but you graced me with life to see another day, and I thank you so much, Lord.

January 7th

God, you have been my everything! My help, my life, my friend. Thank you for being there for me in every possible way. I can't thank you enough. I love you Lord, and I'm truly thankful to have you in my life.

January 8th

God, you are an on-time God, indeed!
Making ways when the time is right,
and not a minute earlier. Thank
you for who you are Jesus. A good
Father to me, you look out for me
every time, and I'm so thankful.

January 9th

Thank you, Lord, for your traveling mercies today. For keeping me from harm, and danger seen and unseen. Along the highways and byways, you kept me while I traveled. Thank you for your grace and mercy.

January 10th

*Your blessings are more than
enough. I thank you today
for my health and strength.
I need you, Jesus, today and
always. Thank you so much.*

January 11th

Lord, you are faithful indeed. Thank you for sustaining me by your Holy Spirit. Allow my life to be pleasing to you, and take away the things that are not pleasing, so that I can honor you in all I say and do.

January 12th

*Thank you, Lord, that when I'm
distracted, you love me still.
When things come into my life
that I'm not expecting, you love
me still. Thank you, Lord, for
your Love. I will praise you always
regardless of my circumstances
or what I'm facing because, God,
you deserve all the praise.*

January 13th

Thank you, Lord, for the grace you've shown my family. Thank you for keeping them and showing them favor. May they always put you first, Lord. I'm nothing without you, and they need you like I need you. Thank you for keeping them, Lord.

January 14th

*My God, you are a wonder
to me! You are so good, and
I thank you for your keeping
power today. I love you, Jesus.*

January 15th

Thank you, Lord, for the grace to
pray this morning. Sometimes
I don't want to get up and pray, but
when I think of how good you are
to me, I can't turn my back on you.
I had to get up and pray. Thank you
for your love and faithfulness.

January 16th

Thank you, Lord, for encouraging my heart through your Word today. Things that people see as insignificant are of great importance to you. Two things came to mind in this instance the widow's mite and your word which states to not despise small beginnings. I thank you for the small things in my life. May I never take them for granted. I love you, Lord, and thank you for the work of the Holy Spirit that brings the truth.

January 17th

Lord, thank you for peace and not turmoil. Your peace in my life is priceless! I'm forever grateful for your peace.

January 18th

Glorious Father, I can't understand your amazing love for me! I don't need to because it's too vast for my little mind to understand such love. I just know that you do, that it's real, and I love you. Thank you for loving me so much.

January 19th

This morning I rise with joy in my heart to bring pleasure to your heart simply because you have created me. I love you and thank you for creating me, Lord.

January 20th

Thank you, Lord, for your love, your grace, and mercy. I can't live without you. I need you every second, every minute, and every hour of every day. Give me a deep desire to spend time reading your word and praying daily. Thank you, Lord, for this desire.

January 21st

Jesus, I thank you. Oh, how I thank you for loving me and allowing me to know you intimately even though I'm flawed. Your righteousness makes me sweet, kind, and loving. Thank you for your sweet Presence in my life.

January 22nd

*Praise God from whom all blessings
flow! Thank you for your promises
that bless my life. You promise
to provide and meet every need.
Thank you for food, water, shelter,
clothing, and finances. Thank you
so much for meeting all my needs.*

January 23rd

Thank you, Lord, for your divine protection over me and my household. I praise you, for you're worthy of all the praise.

January 24th

Thank you, Lord, for your amazing grace! You showed me grace in so many ways today. I could've been hurt in a car accident, but you showed me grace, and I'm so thankful Lord for your protection over me.

January 25th

Thank you, God, for your joy
and presence that fills my soul.
You are truly an awesome
God. Have your way in me.

January 26th

A day without you is lonely indeed.
Thank you, Lord, for your presence
that surrounds me. People around
me or no people around me,
I'm so happy and thankful for
the joy and peace that radiate
my soul. Thank you, Lord.

January 27th

*Jesus, I love to whisper your sweet
Name. You are my everything!
I can't function on any level
without you, Lord. You are mine
and I am yours, and I thank you for
choosing me to be your daughter.*

January 28th

I thank you for all you have done for me, Lord. I haven't seen all that you will do yet, but when I look back over my life, Jesus, I just want to say thank you for always being there for me.

January 29th

Lord, I feel so disappointed today. I feel as though I have abandoned you. Forgive me for my slothfulness, complacency, and lukewarmness at times. I don't want to be like this, yet there are times that I am. Forgive me when I fall short, Lord. Renew your fervent Spirit in me, a fire in my bones for you and the things of God. Thank you for your forgiveness, your patience, and compassion towards me. I appreciate you so much.

January 30th

*Thank you, Lord, for the power
of the Holy Spirit living in me.
He's with me daily through all my
endeavors. I'm thankful that He will
never leave nor forsake me. Thank
you, Lord, for your faithfulness.*

January 31st

Lord, in you I put my trust. In you,
I get up and walk every day by faith.
Thank you, Lord, for ordering my
steps because I don't know which way
to go, and I thank you for leading me.

February 1st

February is the month that the world shows love. Valentine's Day is on everyone's mind, and they go all out to display it to their significant other. Your love tops them all. Thank you for your love that draws me close to you and you to me. You paid a hefty price at Calvary to show me how much you love me, and I'm so very thankful for your sacrifice.

February 2nd

I thank you for this day. A day that I will never see again. Help me to appreciate the beauty of this day and for making me the person you created me to be.

February 3rd

Lord, give me a passion to put you first in my life. To put you first before myself, spouse, children. My desire is to put you first. Thank you, Lord, for doing this in me.

February 4th

*Thank you, Jesus, for life, heath, and
strength today. You are a good God,
and I thank you for everything.*

February 5th

It's great to have life. I spoke with someone, and later I heard that they had passed away. Lord, thank you for allowing me to take the time to converse with this individual. Neither of us knew that it would be the last time we spoke to each other, but you did! Thank you for not being too busy to say hello to people. I cherish the life you give me, Jesus, and I thank you for this special, one-time gift called life.

February 6th

Help me, Lord, to put you first
each day. Don't let me take you
or your goodness for granted,
Jesus. Thank you, and I love you
for transforming my life into what
you have created me to be.

February 7th

*Great is your faithfulness. I long
to be faithful like you, Jesus. May
I demonstrate faithfulness
throughout my daily walk with you.
Thank you, Lord, for doing this in me.*

February 8th

Blessings, glory, honor, and power forever to your name, oh Lord! You are the keeper of my soul, the lifter of my head, and I love you. Thank you for your goodness. You are truly a great God, and I praise you.

February 9th

Jesus, you are majestic! Thank you for watching over me and my family. Order our steps each day and keep us from drifting. Thank you, Lord, for your goodness.

February 10th

Jesus, I love you because you are
so amazingly perfect. I'm glad
that you know me. You know
my heart and my motives, and
I thank you for loving me.

February 11th

God, you're awesome in all your ways.
I thank you for your sovereignty.
You're in control of all things. I'm
secure in you and with you. I'm so
glad that you're God, and no one else
is God or can be God. You're God all
by yourself and I love that about you.
Thank you for being Almighty God.

February 12th

My Father, Abba. Your promises keep me going each day. Without them, life would be futile, but thanks be to the living God of Abraham, Isaac, and Jacob, the God I serve, that you have made me glad in my life, and I thank you, Jesus, for being all things to me.

February 13th

Glory to God! Hosanna to God in the highest! You are awesome, Lord Jesus. Awesome beyond words. You're sweeter than honey in the honeycomb, and I love you. Let my love for you not be with words only but with action and deeds. Thank you, my Creator, my Savior, and my Friend.

February 14th

Today is the day everyone tries to show Love. Your Valentine's Day to me and this world is demonstrated in John 3:16, as well as 1 Corinthians 13. Lord, you have the perfect agape love for people, and I love you for the love that you gave me, and your love that will never ever change.

February 15th

Jesus, sweet Jesus, thank you for the ability to make choices. Every choice, good or bad, has consequences, and I thank you for your Holy Spirit who gives me guidance and direction to choose correctly when there are decisions to be made. I thank you for your help in all things.

February 16th

Thank you, God, for the opportunity to accomplish and do the things that I do, even when I feel inadequate. I'm only able to do these things that take me out of my comfort zone because you have graced me by your Spirit to do them. Thank you, Lord, for helping me to accomplish each task. Through my fear and nervousness, you were there. You didn't leave me but empowered me to do what I could've never done by myself had it not been for your presence. Thank you, Lord.

February 17th

Thank you, Lord, for the ability to shine some light and encouragement to a young lady today. May her joy be full today, Jesus. Thank you for helping me to reach out to her and to make her day more beautiful. To your Name be the glory, Jesus.

February 18th

Thank you, Jesus, and glory to your Holy Name. Thank you for your Holy Spirit who keeps me walking by faith. Thank you for your love, power, and strength that gives me victory over the enemy.

February 19th

*What a wonderful thing it is
to have sweet fellowship with
the Lord. Thank you, Lord, for
relationship with you, and thank
you for making yourself real to
me. I value our relationship, Jesus.
Teach me each day to walk closer
alongside you. I'm grateful for you.*

February 20th

It is a pleasure to serve you and to serve others. You made me to worship you and to serve others. You came to serve us Lord, and I thank you for the opportunity to serve.

February 21st

Thank you, Lord, for a day of rest.
Just like you rested after your work,
you gave us off days to rest as well.
Self-care is important so we can
care for our bodies—our temples.
Thank you for times of refreshing.

February 22nd

Thank you for a sound mind. It helps me stay on task and work effectively each day. I give you praise, Lord, and pray that those whose health has been challenged will experience restoration in Jesus' name. Thank you so much for my sound mind.

February 23rd

*Thank you, Lord, for new mercy
and grace this morning. To be
alive, to pray for others, and
to enjoy the beauty of all your
creation. Thank you so much.*

February 24th

Thank you, God, for your favor on my life.
Where can I go, Lord, without you? Nowhere!
I need you; I want you; I love you, and I will
always be grateful to you. You are my life,
my everything. I'm glad to know you as my
Lord, my Savior, my Redeemer, my Deliverer,
my Healer, my Waymaker, and my Friend.
Thank you, Lord! I can't thank you enough.

February 25th

Blessed assurance, Jesus is mine. You are mine, and I am yours. You bought me with a price, your precious Blood. Thank you, Jesus, for dying for me. For dying in my place. Thank you for taking the fall for me. For taking my sins and giving me your righteousness. Thank you, God, for the gift of salvation, and the presence of your Spirit living in me. Thank you always.

February 26th

Thank you, Holy Spirit, for empowering my life to serve you. I can do all things because of your strength in me. Continue to order my steps each day. I love you God the Father, God the Son, and God the Holy Spirit.

February 27th

To God be the glory and bless
your Holy name. Thank you for
using me and trusting me to be a
servant of the most High God.

February 28th

*Thank you, God, for all you are doing,
all that you have done, and all that
you will do in my life, in Jesus' name.
I appreciate it all, and I'm so grateful.*

March 1st

*I thank you for the gifts and talents
you have given to me, Lord. You
are wise, the Ancient of days,
and I enjoy loving, praising, and
thanking you, Lord. I thank you,
God, for making me in your image,
and I will forever delight in you.*

March 2nd

Thank you for the ability to walk in your way. It can be challenging at times, but the Holy Spirit takes me through every challenge. I love that about you. I can make it and have victory because of your grace. I adore you, Jesus.

March 3rd

I have tasted and seen that you are good, Lord. You are good to me, and I'm thankful that your love for me will never fail. It goes on, and on, and on. Thank you so much, Lord.

March 4th

This day is special because it was the day you chose for my mom to be born. I thank you for my mom. It was she who taught me about you, Jesus, and demonstrated by her example how I should live for you.

March 5th

Thank you for each day. When it's hot, too cold, or raining, I thank you. Thank you for giving me a heart to find the good in everything.

March 6th

*Lord, I give you praise because
I have breath in my lungs to praise
you. Thank you for your breath in
me. I couldn't say another word
if it wasn't for your grace that
gives me the ability to breathe.
It's all because of you and I just
want to say thank you.*

March 7th

Thank you, Lord, that what I do for you and the Kingdom is good work. I give you the praise for helping me to persevere in the things of God, knowing that your reward is great, and my labor is not in vain.

March 8th

Who is like you, Lord? I thank you for your love, your wisdom, and faithfulness. You are a Wonder. I thank you that there is no one like you. I can depend on you with every fiber of my being, and that's comforting.

March 9th

Jesus, my heart is comforted by who you are. My soul finds peace in you, and I'm happy about it! I love you Jesus, the Redeemer of my life. Oh, what a joy to have this reality! Thank you, Lord.

March 10th

Thank you, Lord, that I'm complete in you. Your word declares that I'm fearfully and wonderfully made, and I'm just delighted to know that I'm forever beautiful because you made me in your image.

March 11th

God, thank you for the desire in
my heart to thank you. One leper
returned to thank you, and you
inquired about the other nine.
May I always give you thanks like
the one leper who returned.

March 12th

*Being grateful wears on me like a
garment. I sometimes cry because
I'm so thankful for everything, Jesus.
My heart is filled with gratitude
and thanksgiving unto you.*

March 13th

*There are no words to express
my feelings for you. No words to
express my thanks. I thank you
for the Holy Spirit who expresses
my feelings to you in a way I'm
unable to do. I love you, Lord.*

March 14th

Help me to walk in the Spirit
daily praising you and giving
you thanks along life's journey
as you order my steps, Lord.

March 15th

I got up today and looked up to the sky to see your creation. The sun came out of your mouth. You spoke it into existence. That sun is tangible proof that you are real because no one could hold the hot sun in his/her hand to place it there. Thank you for your creation that gives us light and warmth.

March 16th

*Lord, thank you for knowing me
in the most intimate way. Even
the hairs on my head you have
counted, and it's beautiful and
comforting at the same time that
nothing is too hard for you.*

March 17th

I'm running out of adjectives and words to describe you and thank you, but that's why you are God and no one else is. You are so vast, and eternity still wouldn't be enough to thank you. I love you, Lord.

March 18th

Sovereign Lord, I thank you. The
God of the entire universe, I thank
you. You change not and what you
say stands forever. I thank you for
holding everything in your hands.
Thank you, my triune God. You
gave me so much joy and peace.

March 19th

Thank you, God, for a church home, for community, and for a place to worship with leaders after your heart. Thank you for a place where I can go and be restored, revived, refreshed, and built up to continue this Christian journey.

March 20th

All of my help comes from you, Lord. Thank you for being here for me. Even when I can't feel your presence, you're with me. I depend on you. I trust you. You can never fail, and that's 100 percent guaranteed. What a wonderful fact! My sweet Jesus, your daughter is happy to know that she can rest in you at all times.

March 21st

Thank you, God, that I can make
a difference. I love that your grace
and mercy will follow me all the
days of my life, to aid me in being
a help to all those I meet.

March 22nd

Good morning, Lord! Thank you for
the opportunity to pray for others.
Thank you for praying through me.
I am humbled that I am a chosen
vessel that you use to pray for
others. Thank you for using me.

March 23rd

Thank you, Lord, for your patience and long-suffering towards me. You put up with my faults, my mistakes, and with the times I'm not faithful. Mankind would have given up on me or cut me off a long time ago. I'm so glad that you are who you are, and no one else is you, Lord. Thanks for being compassionate and patient towards me.

March 24th

Thanking you, Lord, will take a lifetime. I love you. What you have done for me is overwhelming. Thank you for seeing me when others don't.

March 25th

Thank you for your sacrifice. Your death gave me life. I am just grateful.

March 26th

Who loves me? Who cares for me?
Who sacrificed for me? You did
all of the above. All the time, it's
you, Jesus, and I thank you.

March 27th

Thanks for rising from the grave!
What freedom that one act
brought. It can never be copied.
You are the first and the last.
I rejoice with glee because your
act of love made me more than a
conqueror. Thank you so much.

March 28th

Another day to wake up and praise you. Another day to sing of the goodness of your love. I can't live without you, and I'm grateful that you made a way so that I don't ever have to live separated from you.

March 29th

God, you are a burden bearer. When
bad news comes my way, I can lean
on you, pray to you, and trust your
promises because you are never
ever defeated. You are always
victorious. I thank you for victory.

March 30th

Love is a beautiful thing, and Lord,
you are Love. Bless your name
for gracing me with your love.

March 31st

God, I thank you daily for giving
me life. I will live for you with
all my being. My heart is full
of gratitude and thanksgiving
for all that you have been in
my life. Glory to your name.

April 1st

*This day is known as All Fools
Day. The fool says in his heart
that there is no God. I thank you
for giving me the sense to know
that you do exist and that you
are my only hope in this world.*

April 2nd

Teach me, Lord, to walk faithfully
before you, to revere your name,
and to worship you with all my
heart, mind, and soul. I thank you
that it is you who enabled me to do
this each day, and I am thankful.

April 3rd

Thank you, Lord, for your undying love and mercy towards me. I wouldn't know what to do had it not been for your grace and mercy. You have kept me from so many things known and unknown, and I give you thanks with a grateful heart this day.

April 4th

Praise the Lord for the word of God.
It is a lamp to my feet and food to
my soul. I thank you for your Holy
Spirit that kept me yesterday,
that is taking care of me now and
will take care of my tomorrows.

April 5th

*All good things come from you,
Jesus, and it's wonderful to know
that when bad comes, only you alone
have the power to work the bad for
the good. It is truly a blessing to
know this truth. Thank you, Lord.*

April 6th

Thank you, Lord, for your
unadulterated word that comes
forth and speaks to my heart. It
brings change to my life. Help
me not only to hear it but to walk
in it, do it, and practice it so
I can be transformed into your
image. You are so good to me.

April 7th

Thank you, Lord, for your showers of blessings overtaking me and my household. Showers of blessings that will help me to be a blessing to others. Thank you, Jehovah Jireh. You are my Provider. Nothing that I have compares to you, Lord. My mind cannot fathom the greatness that is on its way in my life, my household, and my church. To your name be the glory now and forevermore.

April 8th

Lead me by your spirit in the way you want me to go. Thank you for allowing me to yield to your guidance so you can control my life to bring me into your divine plans and purpose for my life. To your name be all the glory.

April 9th

Your promises never fail, Lord.
They are always fulfilled. Thank
you for your faithfulness each day.

April 10th

Surely the presence of God is
here. I feel you loving me, caring
for me, guiding me, and I'm so
very thankful for your love.

April 11th

Another day to give you the highest praise. Hallelujah to the King of Glory. Thank you for your goodness and for keeping me in the land of the living. With so much hurt, suffering, and killings, I thank you for another day to fulfill your purpose for me.

April 12th

*I want to shout from the mountain
tops that I am grateful, Jesus!
Grateful for your love, your peace.
Grateful for all the fruits of the Spirit
that you have added to my life. May
your Holy Name be blessed forever.*

April 13th

Great things you have done, Lord.

Your name is powerful, Jesus,

and it is above every ailment,

every injustice, and every manner

of thing that exists on earth,

below earth, or in heaven. I love

you, Sovereign God. My life is in

great hands, and I thank you.

April 14th

*I aim to please you, Lord, in all my
doing. Give me the wisdom to get
understanding, and to serve you
as I walk in your spirit each day.*

April 15th

Your blessings are constant in my life,
and I pray that contentment in the
things of God will continue to be my
portion. I love you, Jesus, and thank
you for all you have done for me.

April 16th

I hunger and thirst after you, Lord. May my appetite for you increase. There are so many distractions along this journey, and I get thrown off the path occasionally, but keep me hungering after you, I pray, in Jesus' Name. Thank you for allowing me to stay connected to the Vine so that I can flourish and grow in you.

April 17th

This journey that I'm on with you is constantly changing. Some days there are ups and other days, there are downs. One thing remains, though—you never change. You are constant and steady. I love that about you and thank you for being the One whom I can depend on.

April 18th

You reign Supreme, and it's amazing
how kind, compassionate, and loving
you are to me. I can't understand
the depths of your love but I'm
grateful for it on every level.

April 19th

To God be the glory. Every day I lift my heart and my hands to offer you praise. There is always something to thank you for, Jesus. Even on the bad days, I can still thank you. You are all good, and I give you total praise.

April 20th

*Thank you, God, for creating
me. You made me who I am,
and I love to praise your name
and give you thanks. I love the
person you are making me into.*

April 21st

Thank you that you are my peace.
You are my peace in every storm.
I'm anchored to you during the
storms, held by your anchor
of love. Thank you for holding
me through life's storms and
keeping me from drifting away.

April 22nd

Gracious God, your name is
wonderful and marvelous, and
I love your name, Jesus. You are
my all-powerful, all-knowing
God. Thank you for all that
you are and so much more.

April 23rd

Thank you for those closely connected to me. Thank you for my siblings, my parents, my sons, and my husband. I also thank you for my family and friends. Thank you for every relationship you have brought into my life. May I be a godly example before them so that they will also know you and give your name praise.

April 24th

Jesus, my protector, my defender,
my all in all. I find security in you.
You keep me from so many things,
and I'm secure in your loving
kindness and your covering.

April 25th

*This day is special. It's the day
I celebrate my wedding anniversary
every year. Thank you for my
spouse. Thank you for giving
me a provider who gets up daily
and provides for me and his
family. Thank you for everything.
Thank you for my marriage.*

April 26th

My hope is in my God. The lover of
my soul. I can do nothing without
you. Thank you for gracing me
with your strength today, Lord.
When I am weak, you are strong.

April 27th

Bless the Lord oh my soul, and all that is within me bless your Holy name. Thank you for your power to heal, power to save, power to restore, and power to change. Who can match your power? No one can! Thank you for being the Great I Am, and I love you.

April 28th

Your presence is welcome here,
Lord God. In your presence there
is fullness of joy. You give me
unspeakable joy, and I'm thankful
that I can smile because of the joy you
have placed deep down inside of me.

April 29th

I magnify and exalt your Name, Jesus.
You are worthy of praise. I thank you
because when trouble comes you are
a present help that I can depend on.
I give you praise because you never
disappoint. You always come through
for me in your time, and not my own.

April 30th

Mighty fortress, clothed in strength,
Lion of Judah, I thank you and
praise you for your Supernatural
works and power. No one can beat
you, fool you, or destroy you, and
on top of all that, you are my God!
Thank you, Abba. I do love you so.

May 1st

I think of the song that was sung at Harvest when I was growing up. Especially, the part of the song that said, "All good things around us are sent from Heaven above, so thank the Lord, oh thank the Lord for all is good". No truer words. God shines his light on the just and unjust, and he makes all things well for those He created. I thank you from the bottom of my heart, Lord, for your provision.

May 2nd

Thank you for leaders that I can look up to. Leaders from my youth, like my parents, grandparents, teachers, and pastors. Thank you, Lord, for placing them in my life. However, my greatest leader is my mom, who guided me and taught me the things of God. She gave me a solid foundation, and I'm so grateful to you for my mother.

May 3rd

Lord, your word lives forever. Cause it to spring up inside of me like a river. Thank you for your word that brings remarkable change. Hallelujah.

May 4th

Father God, love is so very important. The greatest gift is love, and you gave that gift to me and the world by sending your only Son to shed his Blood for me. Thank you, Jesus, for this once-in-a-lifetime, precious gift.

May 5th

From the foundation of the world
you had a plan for my life. Plans to
prosper me, not to harm me, but
to give me hope and a future. Your
word is true, and your promises
are yes and Amen. Thank you
for all your plans for my life.

May 6th

I am content with you, Jesus.

You are the true and living God.

There is no darkness in you and no

imperfections, either. You are perfect

in all your ways. Pure, Holy, and True

are you, Lord, and I give you thanks.

May 7th

Since the foundation of time,
you established praise. I love to
praise your name and to thank you
because you are so worthy. I sure
do love to praise your name.

May 8th

Thank you, Lord, for the women in my life.
My mom and sister are very special to me.
I love them with an everlasting love. They
have been my supporters and my best friends.
I can lean on them at any time, and they
will be there for me. I don't take that lightly.
Neither do I take them for granted. Thank
you, Jesus, for giving them to me, and me
to them. I really appreciate you, Lord.

May 9th

Thank you for your sweet, gentle spirit, Jesus. You have given me that spirit, as well, and I'm grateful to have that inner strength and gentle spirit that you have bestowed on me.

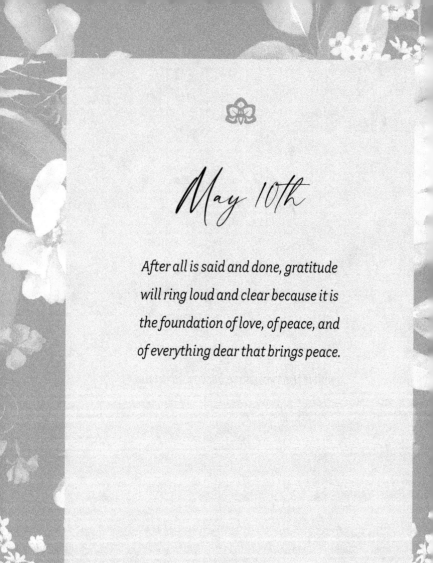

May 10th

After all is said and done, gratitude will ring loud and clear because it is the foundation of love, of peace, and of everything dear that brings peace.

May 11th

Your banner over me is love,
and I thank you sincerely for
your steadfast love, Jesus. It is a
banner that I wave with pride in
my walk with you. Let your love
forever shine through me.

May 12th

Lord, you never sleep or slumber. You
watch over me every night and keep
me in safety. You never miss a beat.
You are always the night watchman
hovering over me. Thank you for your
protection. You are so amazing.

May 13th

Lifting up the Name of Jesus this morning. Shouting and praising Him because He is the water in a thirsty land, the food in famine, and the Way Maker when I can't see the way. Thank you, Lord!

May 14th

Lord, I don't know what lies ahead
or what tomorrow holds but you
do, and because of that, I rest
peacefully and soundly in you.
Thank you that my future, dreams,
and destiny are all in your hands!

May 15th

God, I thank you for faith. For faith to trust you in every circumstance. Thank you for your gift of faith and your anointing of the Holy Ghost.

May 16th

The King of Glory loves me. How awesome is that? The one that made heaven and earth loves me. Can you believe He's in love with me? With you? With us? Praise your Holy name, Jesus, and thank you so much for your love.

May 17th

I adore you, Jesus. I thank you,
for you are undeniably good,
wholesome, and sweet in every
single one of your ways.

May 18th

Lord, I'm encouraged today. Thank you for bringing to fruition all that you will for my life, my sons' lives, and my spouse's life. Thank you.

May 19th

Traveling down this path of life with you, Lord, is unique in every way. Sometimes I wonder why this, or why that, and you patiently hold me up until I can see why this or why that. Thank you for your patience with me. You care so much for me, and I don't have enough tongues to thank you.

May 20th

Throughout every season of my life, you have been there, Lord. On the mountains and in the valleys, you have been there. In my comings and goings, you have been there. Just like my shadow never leaves me, you don't either, and I can't help but say thank you.

May 21st

Thank you, Lord, for fun days. Days when I can lay aside all the cares of the world and have fun. Thank you for those times of leisure where I can laugh my head off, sing, and dance. Days where I can enjoy family and close friends. These are days that mean the world to me, and I thank you for each day like this.

May 22nd

*Joy comes in the morning. Some
days are sad, like the passing of a
loved one. I thank you that you are a
comforter who can sympathize with
my pain. You soothe the yearning in
my soul and substitute great peace.
What a loving Savior you are.*

May 23rd

Lord, you are majestic in all your
ways. I worship you. There is no
one like you, no one before you or
after you that offers such quality
in servanthood. Oh, Majesty,
I worship and thank you.

May 24th

Who is the King of Glory? The
Lord, strong and mighty. You
have kept me from the fiery darts
of the enemy, kept me from the
snares and traps of the enemy,
and I rejoice in you because you
are the keeper of my soul, my
deliverer, and my victorious One.
Thank you, Lord, that no weapon
formed against me shall prosper.

May 25th

Jesus, I thank you for being there for me. I can tell you all my secrets, share my whole heart with you, and you wouldn't tell anyone my secrets. I can be real with you, vulnerable with you, and you love me just the same. Thank you.

May 26th

Haven't I been good to you? Oh yes, Lord. You have been more than good. I can't thank you enough for your goodness in my life.

May 27th

Thank you for your wisdom and understanding in caring for those you allowed to cross my path. May I be your hands and feet to those who may need help, and may I be a listening ear for those who just want someone to hear their plight.

May 28th

God, I thank you for helping me to love those who are hard to love. Some people are just plain mean, and only your spirit will help me to love them. I recall working with an individual who was mean to me for the entire time on the job. I had a choice to leave or to be mean right back, but I chose to turn the other cheek because doing so would please you. Thank you for seeing me through that difficult season, and for allowing me to bring glory to your Name.

May 29th

Thank you, Lord, for empathy, compassion, and love. These qualities are hard to find in people sometimes. You were compassionate. May I walk in these virtues and bring change to those I meet along my journey.

May 30th

Thank you for freedom, Lord. There
is freedom in serving you. I have been
set free from bondage because of you,
Lord, and I'm so grateful for this.

May 31st

The greatest man who ever lived loves me. Thank you, Lord, for giving me a sense of accomplishment each day. I get up with joy in my heart and a pep in my step, and it's all because of you and your amazing grace.

June 1st

Thank you, Lord, that when I'm faced with the impossible, you are there to remind me that with you all things are possible. I can see that nothing is too hard for you when I read how you made a way for Moses through the Red Sea and how you saved Daniel from the Lion's den. You were that God then, and you are that God now. Thank you that all things are possible to those who believe, and Lord, I believe!

June 2nd

I'm complete in you. My identity is in you. I find great joy in knowing that I don't have to compare myself to others but simply look to you to guide me by your truth, and I thank you that doing this makes me whole in you.

June 3rd

Obedience is better than sacrifice. Help me, Lord, to choose to obey and not delay when there is a reason to act. Thank you for allowing me to overcome fear and to step out in faith, courage, and boldness of the Holy Ghost.

June 4th

*I am just a servant, Lord, willing
to serve you in spirit and in
truth. I wake up each day just
praising you for your goodness.
It is with joy that I thank you.*

June 5th

There are days I get up with pain. Thank God it's not all the time! Sometimes, it's pain in my shoulder, pain in my knee, or a headache, but praise be to God that I can call on Jesus because He is my Healer who made my healing a done deal way back at Calvary.

June 6th

Patience is a virtue. In this microwave world where everyone expects things to be accomplished in seconds, it's good to grow in patience. Sometimes in traffic, in long lines at grocery stores, we tend to get impatient. I'm no exception. God, I thank you for teaching me to wait for your timing. Not to fret but wait with joy, and I thank you.

June 7th

Thank you, Lord, that I am okay when I am with people and I'm okay when I'm alone. I'm fine when they love me, and fine when they don't. I'm content with myself and this is freeing because no one can make or break me—whatever decisions are made by myself or others, I'm okay. I am a winner. I'm victorious regardless of the circumstance. Thank you so much for this freedom, Lord.

June 8th

Thank you every moment for who
you are, Father. I am grateful
that you are my source in life and
that you never go on empty or run
out of anything that I need.

June 9th

God, you are full of compassion. It's needed so much in today's world, but instead we just see harshness from those who are not caring at all. Help my heart to always have love and compassion, to care for others. Thanks be to the living God.

June 10th

Thank you that when I go to bed, you allow me to sleep peacefully. Some people can't sleep. Their minds are burdened and heavy laden. Some battle insomnia. Give them peace, Jesus, and lighten their load. Help them to cry out to you. Thank you, Father.

June 11th

Thank you for information coming though social media, television, books, and by mouth about who you are. I pray that information spreading across the world will tell people of your Love, and not lift up lies and hatred that seems to be spreading like a wildfire. May people seek the truth of your word. Thank you, Lord.

June 12th

It's always a challenge to be kind when others are unkind. Thank you, Sovereign Lord, for shining your light through my life so kindness will be modeled for others to see.

June 13th

Don't give up on love people
because God is Love. I thank Him
for helping me to love through
the good, bad, and ugly.

June 14th

*Thank you for making a way
when I couldn't see how things
will work out. I prayed and you
responded with peace over ever
situation. Thank you, Lord.*

June 15th

*I thank you, Lord, for putting a song
in my heart. I love to sing praises
to you, and singing to you brings
your presence and tremendous joy.*

June 16th

Thank you, God, for your great works and marvelous deeds! You are awesome in this place, and I thank you.

June 17th

*I fall short every day, and
I just want to say thank you
for your mercy. That's all.*

June 18th

Your everlasting love and kindness is what I live for. It is the source of my strength.

June 19th

Thank you, Jesus, that when I'm weary, I can find strength in you. Renew my strength like an eagle so I can run on for you.

June 20th

I'm grateful for all you've done.

Keep me, Jesus, as I continue

to serve and thank you.

June 21st

I give my talents and gifts to you
because they belong to you. I'm just
a steward of them, and I thank you
for trusting me with these gifts.

June 22nd

*Each day brings an opportunity to
make a difference. I yield myself
to you, Jesus, and I thank you.*

June 23rd

Jesus, you're the answer to all of life's problems. Thank you for being the problem solver in my life.

June 24th

*I couldn't have made it if you
weren't on my side, Lord. It is so
good when the victorious God
is on your side. Thank you.*

June 25th

You are solid as a Rock. Those who put their trust in you will not be disappointed. I trust and thank you.

June 26th

Thank you for answered prayer.
I pray; you answer. Sometimes I have
to wait. Other times it's immediate.
Thank you for strengthening my
faith through answered prayers.

June 27th

Living for you has richly

blessed my life. Thank you.

June 28th

When I'm not faithful, you
are. Thank you, Lord, that
you never let me down.

June 29th

Have your way in me. Mold me,

cleanse me, and give me the

desire to love you and worship

you. I give you thanks.

June 30th

The best is yet to come, and
I thank you for that, Jesus.

July 1st

Thank you that you're worthy, Lord.

Continue to move by your Spirit.

July 2nd

Awesome ruler, I'm serving you with a grateful heart. Thank you for the simple things in life.

July 3rd

The joy of the Lord is my strength. Thank you for giving me strength every day.

July 4th

Our nation's independence.
You brought the best freedom
and independence known
to man into reality. Who you
make free is free indeed. Thank
you for making me free.

July 5th

You are in control at all times. Even

when things are out of control,

you are large and in charge. Oh,

how I love this, and thank you.

July 6th

Good morning, Jesus! Thank
you for waking me up this
morning. I have new mercies this
morning to praise you, to make
a difference on this new day.

July 7th

Sometimes I struggle to come in your presence because, like Martha, I'm distracted, busy, and occupied with all kinds of stuff that, though not bad, are not more important than putting you first. Forgive me, Lord, and help me to put you first, in Jesus' name. Thank you for your forgiveness.

July 8th

I'm a daughter of the living God.
He redeemed me and bought me
with a price. Sometimes it's hard
to understand why an Almighty
God would claim me, a mere person
who make mistakes and falls short
daily, but you do because you are the
epitome of love, and I thank you.

July 9th

My heart's desire is to please you, fear you (reverence), and keep your commandments. Holy Spirit, I can only accomplish this with your help each day. I thank you for helping me do this.

July 10th

Thank you for reviving me by your Spirit. Sometimes I get weary on the journey, but I thank you for a "spiritual pick me up," so to speak.

July 11th

Turn on the news and there is always so much sadness. How depressing at times. I thank you that you have overcome the world and everything in it. This brings so much hope and peace, and I thank you for hope in a world of despair.

July 12th

There is no one else who can see
the future except you. People
are drowning in despair and are
unable to see the light at the end
of the tunnel. Some are choosing
to end their lives because they are
surrounded by darkness. Lord,
I thank you for helping them to
see the light and for giving them
hope to live and see another day.

July 13th

Thank you for the latter rain that comes to refresh us all. I know by faith that there is so much in my future that is to come. Things that will definitely blow my mind, because you do great things. That is just who you are! Oh, how I thank you for your greatness, your spirit of excellence, and splendor!

July 14th

Lord, thank you for your grace to pray and intercede for others. I look at the world today, and all hell is breaking loose. Many people are leaving this earth with swiftness! Awaken your people, Lord, so that they may care more and move with an urgency to pray for those who are leaving this earth not knowing you.

July 15th

Without hesitation, God is able to
set the captives free. Give people
faith to trust you, Lord. Give them
hearts to serve you. I thank you
for opening up their hearts and
minds to trust and believe in you.

July 16th

Glory to God in the Highest. Thank you, Lord, that all good things come from you. There was nothing made unless you made it. Thank you for your beautiful creation.

July 17th

When I consider how you provide for the birds of the air and the lilies of the fields, I can't help but trust you to provide for me. You provide everything I need clothes, food, and jobs. I thank you.

July 18th

This is the day that you have made.
I look to find joy, and the good in this
day. I rejoice that I'm alive to praise
you. Bless the Lord that I'm in my
right mind, and I thank you for it.

July 19th

To God be the glory for all the
things you have done. You've
kept my sons, my spouse, my
family, and me today. Thank you,
Lord for your keeping power.

July 20th

Thank you, Lord, for moving in my life. Continue to mold me into the image of your Son. I love you Jesus, and I wholeheartedly thank you.

July 21st

Since the beginning of time, you've had plans for me. I thank you for fulfilling your plans in my life. Help me to stay on the path as you continue to order my steps.

July 22nd

Your benefits in my life are comparable to none. You are a wonderful Savior who desires to give me your best. I am nothing without you, and I thank you for all you are pouring into me.

July 23rd

At your feet, I lay my concerns. At your feet, I wait for your instruction. Teach me to hear your voice clearly before I move. Thank you for helping me to be disciplined in your presence.

July 24th

*My desire is to press toward the mark
of a higher calling. Your sheep know
your voice. Thank you for the process
as I go from glory to glory in you.*

July 25th

May peace, joy, and love be my portion each day. Thank you for your Holy Spirit that will manifest these virtues in my life.

July 26th

My desire is to honor you. Keep me
and I will be kept. I love you, Father,
and I thank you for your faithfulness.

July 27th

Lord, give me grace to diligently
pursue you and grace to seek after
you. Father, I'm appreciative of
you. I thank and love you, Lord.

July 28th

I look to you for all my needs.

I am never without when I call

on you, and I thank you.

July 29th

I adore you and I thank you for
my relationship with you so that
I may know you intimately.

July 30th

The enemy comes to bring confusion,
but you are not a part of his
confusion. Thank you, Lord, that
your word is clear and straight to
the point. God, you are my life.

July 31st

An exercise of daily thanksgiving
is good for my soul. I enjoy
telling you how grateful I am
and how much I love you.

August 1st

The summer months are eagerly welcome after long winters. School is out and families enjoy traveling, sending their kids to camp, etc. I thank you for relationships. They are vital to all people because you said it isn't good for man to be alone. Thank you, especially for my relationship with you.

August 2nd

Nothing happens by chance because there's an appointed time for everything under the sun. May I remember when things don't happen as I expected because it's not the right time and to wait on you. Thank you for this revelation.

August 3rd

Unless God builds a house, we labor

in vain. Help me to do things your

way, by your design and pattern,

and not my own. I want all that

I do for you to stand and to be on a

solid foundation. Thank you, Lord,

for helping me do things your way

because your way is always right.

August 4th

I love to dance, sing, and laugh. I guess I can say that they are my hobbies. Just like reading, taking a walk, and trying to draw (lol), just to name a few. I thank you so much for my personality.

August 5th

God, you are my life. I love you very much. I don't want to say "I love you" loosely, but I want my words, deeds, and lifestyle to demonstrate my love for you. Thank you, Lord, for teaching me how to genuinely love you, my God, my Father.

August 6th

As nights turn into days, and days into nights, the Lord is always there, giving us strength to endure all that the enemy throws at us. Thank you, Jesus, that you are a present help in times of trouble each and every day.

August 7th

Thank you, God, that in you there
is no lack. We come to you with
hearts longing to be filled with
your goodness. My trustworthy
and only Provider, I thank you.

August 8th

May my life be fruitful each day.
Thank you for producing your
goodness and mercy that others can
glean from in their time of need.

August 9th

What a Mighty God you are! You provide for the poor, the widow, and the orphan. Thank you, Jesus, for supplying the needs of those who are often overlooked.

August 10th

Thank you for your favor.
I am grateful for what
you're doing in my life.

August 11th

Show me the way, Lord, for I've never been this way before. You are better than any guide or map; you always know the way because you are the way.

August 12th

It's a wonderful day because it was the day you chose for me to be birthed into this world. I came with a purpose, and I thank you for the greatness that's about to unfold as I'm celebrated yet another year. Thank you!!!

August 13th

During times of grief you are a
comforter, and in times of illness,
you are a healer. You are the great
I AM. Whatever I need you to be,
you are, and I'm happy about
that and very, very thankful.

August 14th

Yesterday is gone; tomorrow hasn't come yet. All I have is now. All I have is today. Thank you for helping me not to get ahead of you, but to walk day by day with you.

August 15th

This day is special because I had my first baby on this date. I became a mom, and you saw me through the birthing process. Thank you for the son you gave me. May he be a blessing to the nations.

August 16th

Thank you, Lord, for keeping me physically, mentally, spiritually, and emotionally. You hold me together like no one can, and it's pure joy!

August 17th

Hallelujah is the highest praise, and
I give you the highest praise this
day because of what you're about to
do for me. I trust and believe you by
faith in all that is yet to be revealed.

August 18th

This God who made us all can be trusted. Just believe and He will work all things for your good. His tender mercy is nothing but love. Thank you, my Lord, for your goodness.

August 19th

I depend on you for everything. Even
the next breath I breathe, I have
to depend on you to inhale and
exhale. My very existence is because
of you. Thank you for the breath of
life that you breathed into me.

August 20th

Your blood never loses its power.
It washes us whiter than snow.
Blood gives life. When it's poured
out, it's death. Your blood poured
out was death for you and life for
me. Thank you, God, for choosing
to lay your life down for me.

August 21st

Since the foundation of the world, you've declared truth. May truth reign in our hearts and lies be silenced so that your people can walk in your truth and not in deception that comes from the enemy. Thank you, Lord, for discernment.

August 22nd

Help me to walk in humility and
not pride. May I always humble
myself before you. I thank you,
Jesus, for doing it in me.

August 23rd

*You say that your sheep know
your voice and follow you. Lord,
sharpen my ears to clearly hear
your voice and follow you. Thank
you for helping me to not be
easily distracted with things.*

August 24th

Let justice reign in this land, let love reign in this land. Eradicate injustice, hate, and racism. Thank you that you are a just God, and your will be done here on earth as it is in heaven.

August 25th

There is nothing new under the sun. Your ways are still the same as they were in generations past. May we exalt you and worship you in the way you desire to be worshiped Thanks so much for teaching me to revere you.

August 26th

God, I thank you for deliverance from every form of bondage. Bring deliverance to those who are oppressed. Break the chains of oppression off every man, woman, boy, and girl in Jesus' name.

August 27th

When I am weak you are strong,
Lord. I boast in your strength, and
how good you are to me. I can't
boast in myself or my best because
my best is like filthy rags as the
word of God declares. Thank you
for your anointing that touches
my life and gives me the ability
to boast in God my Savior.

August 28th

Glory to God for He is a God of power,
riches, and endless love. Thank you
for the God that never changes but
remains constant in love and mercy.

August 29th

Don't give up, people. Hold on
to God's unchanging hand. He
promised to come when we call
on His great name. I thank you
that you hear my faintest cry,
and you come to my rescue.

August 30th

It has been like a breath of fresh air
knowing the Savior. Oh, the joy, the
peace, the love that fills my soul.
I invite everyone to come to the
Savior, for He cares and loves you
so very much. Thank you, Jesus, for
sending laborers on their path.

August 31st

I speak life to everyone in Jesus'
name. Let the love of God be in you
so you can have that abundant life
that God promised all of us. I thank
you for giving me that abundant life.

September 1st

It is often said that diamonds are a girl's best friend, but your truth shows that wisdom is better than diamonds. Thank you for giving me wisdom to understand the ways of life.

September 2nd

In times like these when we feel alone, the Savior gently reminds us to press forward where we trade our loneliness for His purpose. Thank you that you are more than enough.

September 3rd

You are the solution to every
problem. I can come to you when
I'm baffled about things, and you
effortlessly show me the solution
to solve them. Thank you that
there is nothing too hard for you.

September 4th

Continue, Lord, to reveal yourself to me. You are indeed a wonder. You are vast and no one teaches you how to do things. You are supreme and have no equal. Thank you, Lord.

September 5th

One of my favorite hymns is "What a Friend We Have in Jesus."[1] You are indeed a friend to me, and as the lyrics declare, it's a privilege to carry everything to you in prayer. I thank you, Lord, for the privilege to bring my burdens to you in prayer.

1 "What a Friend We Have in Jesus" by Joseph Michael Scriven, 1855, hymnal.

September 6th

Mercy found me, and I rejoice with glee. Knowing without mercy I don't know where I would be. Your mercy is needed everywhere, Lord. Thank you for sowing mercy into my life, so that I can show mercy to others.

September 7th

You orchestrate my life the way you want me to go. You order my steps on a narrow path. I look to you for guidance and for your strength. Thank you for leading me by your Spirit to refresh me in a weary land, oh God. Thank you for your wonderful favor on my life.

September 8th

Glory to God! I love you, Lord, and I thank you for all you have done for me. I'm just amazed at the kind of God you are. You are my everything, and I thank you for your loving kindness towards me.

September 9th

I offer up praise to you this morning,
Lord. In you, I put my trust and wait
for you to guide my day. Thank you
for your plans on this day, and for
everything that this day has to offer.

September 10th

All the days of my life have already been ordained by you, Lord, so why should I fret or why should I worry? Help me to know that nothing or no one can change your plans for my life so that when things go in a direction that I didn't expect, your peace will envelop me. Thank you for being such a magnificent God!!

September 11th

This date was the day God allowed me to be a mom for a second time. It was always a yearly event where family came together to celebrate and sing Happy Birthday until the unimaginable happened in our nation. Thank you, Lord, for keeping us through that awful ordeal. May your presence continue to heal our land, its people, and all who are still suffering from trauma today. It could've been worse, so thank you for your amazing grace.

September 12th

*In your life's ministry here on
earth, you touched those whose
lives were broken. You made their
lives pleasant and complete. You
made them whole, and I thank
you for doing the same for me.*

September 13th

One day, on my brother's birthday, my life was transformed when a prophetic word was spoken over my life. My life continues to unfold as that prophecy has taken root. I thank you, Lord, for your masterpiece, your good work consuming my life.

September 14th

It's baffling when people think that they don't need God. Don't know why I should be baffled though, when I too was just like them before He drew me into a personal relationship with Him. People in general only cry out to God for help when trouble comes. On that day, whether they knew God or not, everyone hollered, "Oh, my God!" His name was called on and lifted up. It shouldn't take a disaster for people to call on God, but I thank you, Lord, that they did.

September 15th

It's so good to give thanks to the Lord.
Your daily provision elicits praise
from the depths of my soul more
deeply than the day before! You're
patient, kind, and gentle. I'm just
so very grateful for all you do that
tears continuously well up in my eyes
because of your goodness to me.

September 16th

Love is a jewel that God has given
to the world through his Son. His
love is priceless, and I'm constantly
thanking you, Father, for your
love. May people everywhere feel
and experience your love, Lord.
It's so much better than hate,
and my prayer is that hate will
be eradicated and love will stand
alone in the hearts of people.

September 17th

Thank you for your righteousness.
Lord, you exchanged my filthiness for
your righteousness. You clothed me
in your righteous garments so I could
be a daughter in your Kingdom.

September 18th

I sometimes feel like just bawling
my eyes out when I think of the
goodness of the Lord. Over and
over again, you love me even more
deeply than the day before. I'm
overwhelmed by your precious love.

September 19th

Thank you for the gift of sight. Where would any of us be without our sight or our other four senses? Our senses play a prominent role in our daily lives, helping us to communicate with you as well as others. When you touched the eyes of the blind man, you touched him twice, and he saw things more clearly. Touch us again, Lord, so that we would see things clearly in the natural as well as spiritually. Thank you for the ability to see the beautiful colors of creation, touch a soft stuffed animal, hear the birds chirping, and taste delicious food. For this, I give you great praise.

September 20th

Thank you for your favor, Lord.
You have favor over me and my
household. I'm truly blessed and
never want to be away from your
presence. May I continue to walk
in the Spirit before you. I can't
keep myself, so thank you for
keeping me, Jesus. I'm appreciative
of all you're doing in my life.

September 21st

Thanks, God, for always working things out for me. It's nice to rest in you and not worry. You're in total control, and you're always working things out behind the scenes. I love serving a magnificent, powerful, awesome God like you!

September 22nd

Worthy is the Lamb! Lord,
remind those who have never felt
accepted on any level that they
are valuable because you made
them valuable. You are a worthy
God who made all things good.
Thank you for allowing them to
find their worth in you, followed
by tremendous joy and peace.

September 23rd

Thank you for your faithfulness.
When I'm not faithful, you are
always faithful. I thank you for
your grace and mercy each day.

September 24th

Some things in life frustrate us to no end, but instead of becoming frustrated, we should breathe and let the frustration go, knowing that what is for us is for us. Lord, thanks so much for reminding me that you are a God of order, and nothing due to us will take place before the time that you have set it to take place.

September 25th

Thank you, Lord, that what you have started in me you will be faithful to complete. May I model patience in waiting on you to perfect all that you're doing in and through my life. I thank you for encouraging my heart today.

September 26th

Thank you, Jesus, for courage.
Help me to be as bold as a lion—
not timid—when I'm tasked with
speaking before people or leading
a group. I shrink away from
stuff like this because it's not my
comfort zone, and I thank you for
empowering me by your Holy Spirit.

September 27th

Come out into deep waters. You
beckoned Peter to get out of the
boat and walk to you. Help my
faith not to waiver when I step out
to do things that I've never done
before. Thank you for helping
me keep my eyes on you.

September 28th

You inhabit the praises of your people. Thank you for a song in my heart to daily praise you. Praise ushers in your presence where there is fullness of joy. I thank you for a tongue to praise you over and over, a voice to sing and shout, and feet to dance to your praises.

September 29th

We all love to have nice things. Homes, clothes, cars, etc. Help me, Lord, to never make material things a god in my life. My identity is in you and never these things. They are blessings that are essential to our day-to-day lives for comfort, but they shouldn't be worshiped. They can all be gone in an instant by natural disasters like floods, earthquakes, tsunamis, landslides, hurricanes, tornadoes, avalanches, and even fires. Thank you for the grace to continue to build my hope in you and nothing less.

September 30th

Thank you for our youth. They are our future. I lift the young people up, and I ask you, Lord, to bring a revival to our youths in this nation and around the world. You said a little child shall lead them. Ignite the hearts of our youth with a passion to know and serve you, God. Thank you by faith for a new generation of leaders.

October 1st

Thank you for balance in my life. Don't allow me to go too far to the left or too far to the right but keep me in balance each day. Too much of anything can be bad for you. For example, if you eat too much candy, honey, or whatever sweet is your preference, you're liable to end up with a tummy ache or headache. Keep us balanced in our thoughts and deeds.

October 2nd

Thank you, Lord, that your Holy Spirit lives by faith in all your sons and daughters. You never, ever compete against yourself. You and you alone is doing the work of the Kingdom in and through them. They don't own anything because everything they have comes from you to enable them to do your work here on earth. I thank you for helping us Christians to see and understand that there is no room for competition among us, no room for us to be territorial, envious, or jealous of each other because none of us own anything.

October 3rd

When we're having a bad day, I'm convinced that if we look hard enough we can find something good to be thankful for. I'm also aware that this is easier said than done, especially for people who may be struggling to make ends meet. Let's say we have an event to attend and outside, it is raining cats and dogs. Instead of grumbling or complaining, we can choose to see the good and be thankful that the rain will help fill our reservoirs, keep us from droughts, and provide crops for our food. Those with difficult circumstances can still find something to be grateful for because there are resources available to assist them. We must all remind ourselves that when we feel that we're doing really bad, there is always someone out there who is doing worse than we are.

October 4th

Thank you for a new day! I woke up with a pain here and an ache there, but I didn't complain. I simply reminded myself that pain is a sign that I'm still here and alive in this world to make a difference.

October 5th

I'm not a fan of going to the dentist. As the appointment day approaches, I become anxious. Perhaps it's the needles or the sound that the drill makes, but whatever the reason behind the anxiety, I wouldn't go at all if I could get away with not going. I just want to thank God for helping me to go even when I am afraid. I go every six months because I don't want to have cavities or gum disease. I often wonder how those six months to see the dentist go by so fast, but my husband's six-month deployments were snail-paced in comparison.

October 6th

Fear can cripple us. God didn't give any of us fear, therefore, we have to choose to rise above every form of fear knowing that as we move forward, fear will lose its grip on us. Thank you, Lord, for giving us the courage to finish every task.

October 7th

Have you ever been looked over, talked down to, disrespected, or misunderstood? I'll say yes for myself and all of you. As long as there's breath in our nostrils, we will face this. It's how we deal with these incidents that make a difference. We can pout, tempers flaring and the like, but that will make things worse, not better. A gentle answer turns away wrath. Say what you have to say, trust God, and watch situations change. Thank you, Lord, for promoting those when others tend to see them as nothing.

October 8th

Life is sacred. It is precious and can be taken in an instant! There are so many deaths around us, and it causes each of us to look at our own mortality. God, help us all to prepare for eternity because on this earth, we're but a vapor. People used to say, "Here today, gone tomorrow," but now, it's more like "Here today, gone today." Every life has been made in your image, and I thank you, Lord, for helping us not to take our lives for granted.

October 9th

In every household garbage is accumulated and tossed out weekly. Like garbage that needs to be tossed out, some people have a lot of accumulated weight placed on them by what others say. Help us all to toss out the garbage in our lives that weighs us down. Help us to toss out what he says or she says. Thank you, Lord, for helping us to embrace what you say, because your words are not burdensome, but they add value to our lives and build us up.

October 10th

*In my God there is strength.
Strength to take me through life's
ups and downs and for anyone
who chooses to trust and believe
God for themselves. Thank you,
Lord, for your anchor that holds
me. I'm truly thankful that you're
holding my life together each day.*

October 11th

I thank you for a gentle spirit.
I thank you for the ability to be kind,
understanding, and gracious to
others. I pray that I will live my life
by the golden rule and treat others
as I would want them to treat me.

October 12th

I love a quiet atmosphere! I enjoy

peace, calmness, and serenity.

Pictures of calm waters and the

sun reflecting on the water evoke

this quietness as well. I thank you,

Lord, for the still waters in my life.

I love you so much for blessing me

with this gem of quiet peace.

October 13th

Gone are the days worrying about "what if this" and "suppose that." Worrying is futile. It doesn't help anything, and it is not a solution. Thank you, Lord, that you hold my everything. You know what I need before I ask, and you're maturing me each day to set aside worry and trust you.

October 14th

I often wonder why we tend to look back on life with regret. There is nothing any of us can do with the past. We can't unscramble eggs, so help us, Lord, to look forward with hope and trust you to salvage what we have lost. Thank you that only you can restore what we lost, and you make it better than it was before!

October 15th

Celebrate every day of life! Rejoice in who the Lord made you to be. Love yourself and thank Him for the person you are. Thank you, Lord, that I'm uniquely me. I love me, and I thank you for me.

October 16th

Driving in traffic is a lesson of patience indeed.
Sometimes you sit in traffic for a long time, and it
can be irritating. Some people drive on my bumper
and I'm praying the whole time that the car in front
of me doesn't suddenly break, causing me to break
and the car on my bumper to rear-end me. Some
people are so rude on the road. Like I said, it's a lesson
in patience, among everything else. Thank you for
bringing me back home safely from every destination
and for helping me to be an example of patience.

October 17th

My delight is in you, Lord. I'm so
happy to have you in my life. You
have brought so much stability,
joy, peace, and boldness, and
I'm amazed at what you're
doing in me. It's all absolutely
remarkable, and I thank you.

October 18th

You give me life that no one

can. I look up to you, adore you,

love you, and I thank you for

helping me run this race.

October 19th

Lord, you are faithful and I'm striving to be consistently faithful, but I drop the ball more times than I can count. Thank you that despite my human frailty, you understand and love me when I totally miss the mark.

October 20th

Lord, I admire the butterfly, the swan, and the dove. The butterfly represents change, rebirth, and transformation. The swan, with its beautiful white feathers, represents beauty, elegance, and grace, and the white dove is a symbol of peace, purity, and gentleness. All these virtues you have birthed in my life, and I'm so very thankful that you've made these beautiful creatures to be a representation of your goodness.

October 21st

Surely God is able! He's able to see you, me, and everyone else through life's mazes, ditches, traps, and snares. He's able to remove the obstacle, the obstruction, and the opposition that is impeding your way forward. I know He's able and I thank Him today.

October 22nd

We have all experienced sickness. For some
of us, it could've been a simple cold, and for
others, the illness was serious enough to
warrant a stay in the hospital or the ICU. God
is our healer. I have seen Him heal family
members and friends. I thank you, Lord,
for faith to believe in you and your healing
power. May we all exercise that mustard seed
of faith and trust you for the miraculous.

October 23rd

Food is essential to nourish our bodies to help us grow. Just like our bodies need food to grow, our spirit needs food to grow, too. Lord, help us to read your word daily so we can be strengthened and nourished in our spirit. I thank you for giving us a hunger for the things of God.

October 24th

Lord, help us to look before we leap. In other words, help us to think of the consequences before we act, because once the act is done, we are unable to reverse it. All our actions, whether good or bad, have consequences, and I thank you, Lord, for giving us the control to think before we do things.

October 25th

Thank you, God, for The Lord's Prayer. As a child, my mom taught me this simple, powerful prayer, and it was also taught to me in Sunday school. There are days when I don't know what to pray or how to pray, and I would say this little prayer from my heart, and it would suffice. It exalts God as my Father, praises Him, and gives reverence to His name. It provides for my daily needs, forgives me, and keeps me from temptation and evil. I pray that everyone will learn this prayer, memorize it, and keep it in their hearts, so that when they need to call on the Lord in prayer, they can have this.

October 26th

I believe you, God. You live in my

heart, and I thank you for allowing

me to know you and to serve you

this day in spirit and in truth.

October 27th

My life is secure in you. I don't have to worry about tomorrow because you've already taken care of my tomorrow. You saw what I would be walking into today when you were on the Cross. I'm just getting to it now, and I thank you for knowing my todays way back then when you hung your head and said, "It is finished!" All my days are complete in you, and I thank you.

October 28th

Thank you, God, that you love us so much that you wouldn't allow us to walk in disobedience. I think of Jonah. He went the other direction, instead of Nineveh, where you told him to go, and as a result, he was swallowed by a whale. Forgive us for being hard-headed. Sometimes we want to have our own way and our own independence. Sometimes we think we know best, but only you know best. When circumstances come, we realize that we too have been swallowed up by a whale of circumstances beyond our control and how much we desperately need you to rescue us.

October 29th

*Just like I can't live without oxygen
to breathe or without water to drink,
I can't live without you, Lord. My life
is in your hands, and I thank you for
creating me and making me yours.*

October 30th

I saw on the news that stealing has become such a problem that store owners are placing items that consumers once retrieved on their own behind the glass, under lock and key. I pray that stealing will end because you command us not to steal. May an honest day's work be everyone's portion, and thank you, Lord, that people would choose to live righteously over ill-gotten gains.

October 31st

Many are celebrating Halloween today. I used to do it until I knew better. Like them, my attraction was getting all that delicious candy! I never liked skeletons, ugly masks, gravestones, or any of the scary stuff, because such things were always associated with evil. However, I didn't care as long as I was getting loads of candy. The lure of candy was my motivation for participating. I often wonder if there was no candy offered whether people still celebrate Halloween. Would they still go to the homes of strangers, dressed in scary costumes, if there were no treats involved? Why or why not? That's something to ponder. Thank you, Lord, for opening our eyes and understanding that there must be more to this than just candy.

November 1st

This is the month when we all celebrate Thanksgiving. Lord, I thank you for your goodness that surrounds me 365 days a year! Your goodness never ends. It pours out to all regardless of their relationship with you. You don't discriminate. You love them all, and I'm grateful that your love never ends.

November 2nd

Thank you, Lord, that as people,
we are valuable. You made us
with gifts, talents, and so much
more! May our gifts be used for
kindness and love towards everyone.
I thank you that we are priceless,
and nothing or no one could have
bought us except the precious
blood of your only Son, Jesus.

November 3rd

Thank you, Lord, that you are a burden lifter. Many are burdened with grief today. I thank you for comforting their hearts and lifting their grief this day.

November 4th

We would not know the price you paid

at the cross of Calvary for our sins

had you not made it known. Thank

you, God, for revelation, wisdom,

and understanding to know who

you are through your word, and for

those servants you sent to convey

the message of the Good News.

November 5th

Jesus, you are the sweet fragrance of love and everything that is needed to beautify our lives. Thank you for being the only One with that distinction—the One who can never ever be duplicated. I love you, Lord.

November 6th

*Trials come daily. Help us to lean on
you when we are faced with trials
of every kind. May we remember
that you have given us victory over
trials and that we have overcome
because of you. Thank you, Lord,
for making us victorious on the
left and right. I give you praise.*

November 7th

Go and tell everyone what God has done for you. Did He wake you up this morning? Tell someone. Did He break the fever you were battling last night? Tell someone. Go and tell someone about His goodness. Go and testify to everyone how good God has been to you. It's testimony time, and I thank you, Lord, for my testimony.

November 8th

Since the day you came into my
life, I've never been the same. I love
you, Jesus, and my prayer is for
others to intimately know you as
well. I thank you for sending people
to speak an encouraging word
to their hearts in Jesus' name.

November 9th

A farmer plants his crops, and then he waits for the harvest to come. Like the farmer, I too have planted a crop and am patiently waiting for my harvest. Thank you, Lord, for allowing me to plant seeds of love, kindness, mercy, and peace. We reap what we sow, and I thank you for a bountiful harvest of your goodness in my life.

November 10th

Certainly, the day is coming when
everyone has to give an account
of what they have said and done
in this life. Help us to live every
day with this truth as a friendly
reminder to let our words and deeds
be helpful to all, never causing
harm. For this, I thank you, Lord.

November 11th

*Born to save, born to love, born
to give hope. I thank you, Lord,
for Jesus, because no one else has
come to do any of this for me.*

November 12th

You reign Supreme! I thank you, Lord, for being dominant over everything and everyone. You are fair, just, and true. Man is not like this. Mankind has favorites; he judges, hurts others, and looks down on the poor. I'm thankful that no one can overthrow you or ever take your place. You are the advocate for all mankind, and I thank you that I can wholeheartedly trust you.

November 13th

Lord, I thank you for humility.
Keep arrogance and pride far from
me. May I humble myself as I walk
with you daily. I'm clay fashioned
by your hands with nothing to
brag about except what you have
done in and through my life.

November 14th

*I am living my life for the One who
gave me life. Daily singing His praises
and remembering where he brought
me from. God, you are my desire, and
I thank you for your hand on my life.*

November 15th

*Glory to the living God who owns
the entire earth and everything in
it! I will never be in lack because
you daily provide for me. I'm
blessed to have you in my life.
Thank you for being my provider.*

November 16th

Wonderful Counselor! Many seek answers to life from others. However, those from whom they seek are extremely limited in what they can do to help them. Thank you, Jesus, that in you are wells of knowledge, wisdom, and counsel. I can come to you with all my problems, and you can solve them all.

November 17th

Thank you, Lord, for adopting
me into your Kingdom. You made
me your own child, just like an
earthly parent would adopt
a child not biologically their
own. You grafted me into your
family and I'm so very glad.

November 18th

Thank you, Lord, that you forgive us of our sins and remember them no more. I'm thankful that when the enemy brings back bad memories, they no longer have the power they once had over us. Thank you for good memories. It's all we have left, especially memories of our departed loved ones. What a joy it is to recall and remember them. Not everyone can recall their memories due to amnesia or Alzheimer's, and for them, I pray for your divine healing.

November 19th

Thank you for meekness. People have a tendency to see meek people as weak or even pushovers. However, nothing could be further from the truth. The Bible described Moses as a meek man, and the Bible said that the meek are blessed and shall inherit the earth. May each of us be graced with this wonderful virtue.

November 20th

Teach us how to respect people's
time and to show up early for
appointments, meetings, or events.
Tardiness is not good. I dislike being
late. I'm sometimes too early, and
this too can be as bad as being too
late. May each of us manage our
time wisely and effectively. Thank
you, Lord, for being an on-time God
who is never too early or too late.

November 21st

Children playing in the park evoke
so much joy. You hear the squeals of
laughter and shouts like, "one more
push!" while on the swings. Give
us that carefree life like children.
They are innocent and trusting.
I thank you for allowing us to be
like children again, so we can lead
others to you with our childlike
innocence and faith to trust in you.

November 22nd

A picture says a thousand words. We
heard the story of the burning bush
where Moses took off his sandals.
That really "drove home" to me when
I visited Sight and Sound and saw
the play "Moses." It unfolded before
my very eyes, just as I had pictured
while reading God's word. Lord,
I thank you for visuals that bring
your message clearly to all people.

November 23rd

It's Thanksgiving Day! Thank you, Lord, for the gift of family, friends, and unity. May every day be a celebration of thanksgiving because of what you've done for us.

November 24th

Some people chase after things that will never bring fulfillment. They chase money and are never happy. They buy flashy cars and are still not fulfilled; they buy diamonds and bigger houses and experience the same results.
I thank you, Lord, that you are the only one who fulfills the longing of our hearts. I'm appreciative and grateful for your presence that brings complete fulfillment in my life.

November 25th

I thank you, God, for manners.
Growing up, we were taught to
say please and thank you, but
it seems to be lacking in society
these days. Grace us all to display
etiquette, good behavior, and
attitude wherever we go, and by so
doing, we will represent you well.

November 26th

King of Kings, Lord of Lords, I thank
you that you will never ever let me
go! I may let go of your hand, but you
will never let go of mine. I may turn
my back on you, but you wouldn't
leave nor forsake me. I thank you
for your powerful grip on my life
and for being my solid rock.

November 27th

Thank you for your Holy Spirit.
He is the still small voice who
keeps me on the right path by
speaking to my heart with truth.
With His guidance, I will never
go wrong. I thank you, Lord.

November 28th

I'm truly thankful for things that
are yet to come. I'm not guaranteed
tomorrow, yet I look ahead by
faith to see what you have for
me. Thank you so much, Jesus.

November 29th

Thank you, Lord, for helping me go the extra mile. Sometimes, it's difficult to do more, but when doing more helps someone, it brings satisfaction to the one going the extra mile and appreciation from the one whom the sacrifice was made for.

November 30th

Look up when you're feeling low;
don't be downcast in spirit, but
look up to the Lord and call on
the Name of Jesus whose ears
are always attentive to those
who are broken. Thank you,
dear Jesus, for your compassion
toward myself and others.

December 1st

All around us are signs of the
approaching Christmas season.
Some homes and trees are already
decorated and beautifully adorned
with twinkling lights. Help us,
Lord, to prepare and adorn our
hearts for you, our coming Savior.
Thank you for coming to earth.

December 2nd

Great is your faithfulness, Lord.
Thank you for being consistent
in my life. You never missed
the mark, dropped the ball, or
failed. You are perfect in all your
ways, and I'm so grateful.

December 3rd

What a mighty God you are! I can't
stop praising your Holy Name
because you keep on blessing
me over and over again. There
are no words nor adjectives that
I can use to describe or thank
you enough, yet I thank you for
honoring my humble efforts.

December 4th

Move away from strife, envy, and
confusion. Don't frequent them
under any circumstances. Instead,
come away with the Lord, the lover
of your soul. Dine with Him and
sup with Him where you will find
peace and rest for your bruised,
hurt soul. Thank you, God, for
being our Sustainer of life.

December 5th

Life can be a rollercoaster or even a merry-go-round. There are just some things in life that take you up and down and around and around for a second time. Help us all to learn the lesson that needs to be learned so we can come out from the vicious cycle that life's journey deals us. Lord, we trade life's merry-go-round for your wheel, the Potter's wheel. I pray you mold us on the Potter's wheel and make us into vessels for your use. Thank you, Lord, for refining and renewing us today so we can ascend to greater heights in you.

December 6th

Merciful Father, thank you for
allowing me another day to come into
your Presence. You are all that I need
from day to day. Without you, there
is no meaning, and I'm so very happy
to be graced with the opportunity
to bow at your feet. Thank you for
hearing my heart's cry and bringing
the longings of my heart to fruition.

December 7th

This morning, Lord, be my hope,
joy, and peace. I have great
expectations of the things I've
prayed for to manifest. I give you
the glory and the praise for all of it
because, without a doubt, neither
who I am nor who I will become
would be possible without you.

December 8th

Most people like to make plans ahead
of time. However, it's God's plans
that always prevail. Lord, help my
plans to agree with the plans you
have for my life. I thank you that
your plans for me are better than
my own, and I fully embrace them.
I thank you and honor you for the
new thing that you're doing in my life.

December 9th

Lord, I thank you for opening
doors to new experiences and new
relationships. Thank you for the
faith to trust and believe you on this
journey. I've never been this way
before, but I'm stepping out in faith
and trusting you as I move forward.

December 10th

As I reflect on my life, I'm thankful that you, Lord, have been the center of it all. Through winnings and losses, you were there; through mourning and laughter, you were there. Even when I wasn't aware of your Presence, I can now see that you have been there all along. Thank you, God, for being the center of my life.

December 11th

The faith walk is not easy, especially
when you're believing for things
you cannot see, but what I do
know is that obedience, believing,
faith, and trust are the ingredients
that make the unseen things a
reality. Lord, thank you for the
faith to see things manifest.

December 12th

When circumstances in life have hurt or disappointed
us, what a blessing it is to still give God praise!
Despite his pain and suffering, Job declared that
"though He slay me, yet will I trust Him!" (Job
13:15, NKJV) He didn't allow his circumstances
to make him forget or turn his back on God,
and neither should we, because God is indeed
faithful. Thank you, Lord, for giving us the ability
to continue to serve you when life is difficult.

December 13th

It is so easy to judge others. So easy to see their imperfections and not our own. Lord, I'm learning not to judge others. Forgive me for the times I have. The word of God encourages us to take the log out of our own eyes before trying to take the speck out of the eyes of someone else. I thank you, Lord, for this biblical principle. I believe that I'm now in a place where I can look in the mirror and critique and judge myself. I thank you for every small step that leads to growth and maturity in my life.

December 14th

Lord, stir up the gifts you put in me
before I was born. Stir up every gift
that is currently lying dormant.
Thank you for your anointing that
enables me to do what I cannot do
on my own. Thank you, Lord, for
a renewed strength, spirit, and
mind. I give you the glory, Jesus, for
what you are going to do, Amen.

December 15th

Many of us work hard and stay up late. We answer everyone's beck and call, stretching ourselves thin, with little to no rest or vacation. Then we wonder why we're burned out or sick. God Himself rested from His work, and we should follow His example and do the same. None of us would run our vehicles without maintenance because eventually the engine would give out, yet we run our bodies to the ground and expect to be well. Thank you, Lord, for granting us the wisdom to take care of ourselves.

December 16th

Giver of life and all things, I thank
you for your faithfulness to me. You
have kept me from my conception
to this day, and I'm appreciative of
the things that only you can do.

December 17th

Never give up on yourself but keep moving forward regardless of how things may appear. Be courageous through the process and surround yourself with those who can lift you up along the journey. Stay far away from naysayers who can dampen your spirit, and remember that God will give you everything you need to be successful in all you do.

December 18th

*All that you have blessed
me with has been noted. I'm
grateful for everything and will
continue to sing your praises as
I travel this journey. Thank you
for being God, and God alone.*

December 19th

Thank you, Jesus, for helping us
to release bitterness, grudges,
and the like. Allow our conscience
to be free from the weight of
unforgiveness. Gird us up with your
truth, so we can walk in freedom
from every form of bondage.

December 20th

Give us room to move when we feel

restricted. Room to come out of our

shells, room to spread our wings

and do new things as we trust you

in new territory. Thank you, Lord.

December 21st

Thank you for being my refuge.
In times of trouble, I can run to
you and be protected. Move by
your Spirit, Lord, to rescue those
in horrific situations. I thank
you for covering them now.

December 22nd

It's you, Lord, that makes all things
bright and beautiful. May your light
shine in the dark places, delivering
those held in captivity by their sins.
Thank you, Lord, for being our Savior.

December 23rd

Sometimes, it's good to let go of
things and quit trying to figure it all
out on our own. To let go and realize
that we can't do it all or know it all.
We thank you, Lord, for knowing that
we can turn it all over to you, and you
will make the things concerning us
plain, simple, and easier to manage.

December 24th

Sometimes we try all we can and do all we can do, and yet nothing changes. Lord, help us during these times to patiently wait on you until the change comes. Thank you for giving us hope while we wait.

December 25th

Thank you, Lord, for another year
to celebrate Christmas. It is my
favorite time of the year! Families
come together, carols are sung,
and gifts are exchanged. We thank
you, Lord, for the blessed Hope,
the gift of Jesus, who brought
peace and goodwill to men.

December 26th

Thank you, God, for true wealth
and prosperity which is found in
your Son, Jesus. May we harness
these riches and carry them in our
hearts so our joy may be full.

December 27th

God, I love you! I say Hallelujah,

which is the highest praise I can give

you. You are worthy of it all, and I'm

so blessed to be able to praise you.

December 28th

I have no idea how I can show
my appreciation to you, Lord.
"Thank you" is all I have, Jesus,
and it is still not enough.

December 29th

Glory to God. I give glory to the
One who came into my life and
left an enduring impression
of Love. Thank you, God.

December 30th

It is well with my soul. You have
given me strength and everything
needed to cement my relationship
with you, and I thank you for the
best relationship over all others.

December 31st

Today is the last day of the year, New Year's Eve, and the curtains are about to come down as the year ends and a new year begins. I thank you, Lord, for seeing me and my family through this year. May next year be filled with greater peace and joy as we continue serving you in Spirit and in truth.

About the Author

Margaret Bernard is a wife, mother of two sons, and a believer by faith. She loves to laugh, pray for others, and volunteer in ministry with the intercessory prayer team at her church. Margaret resides in Virginia Beach, Virginia with her husband.